KU-499-223

THREE THIEVES
BOOK FIVE

Pirates of the Silver Coast

SCOTT CHANTLER

Kids Can Press

ACT ONE

Fortune

6

I HOPE YOU TWO HAVE ENOUGH MONEY TO KEEP RENTING THIS ROOM, BECAUSE I PLAN TO DO NOTHING BUT SCRATCH THIS LEG FOR THE NEXT SEVERAL DAYS!

Scratch
Scratch
Scratch

WE'RE BROKE, AREN'T WE?

I'VE BEEN PICKING POCKETS IN THE MARKET DISTRICT...

...BUT MOSTLY WE'VE BEEN LYING LOW, TRYING TO KEEP OUT OF SIGHT WHILE WE WAITED FOR YOU.

<SIGH>

PENNILESS. LIKE OUR CIRCUS DAYS ALL OVER AGAIN.

8

YEAH. SO IF YOUR PLAN IS TO HIRE A SHIP AND GO TO THIS ISLAND OF ASTAROTH, WE'RE GONNA NEED TO STEAL SOME REAL MONEY...

...OR AT LEAST SOMETHING *BIG* WE CAN SELL.

DESSA...?

YOU OVERHEARD ME TALKING TO—

DID I?

DON'T TOY WITH ME, NORKER.

IF THAT CRYSTAL BALL REALLY WORKS, THEN TELL ME WHAT YOU KNOW. OR I *"DIVINE"* A QUICK PARTING OF YOUR HEAD FROM YOUR NECK.

TUT-TUT, GOOD SIR...

...THAT'S NOT HOW IT WORKS, AND YOU KNOW IT.

FORTUNES TOLD

1 SHILLING

WHUMP

Plunk!

VERY
WELL.

15

16

I'M LOOKING TO HIRE A SHIP.

SAILORS CAN BE DANGEROUS COMPANY, MISSY. THE SEA AIN'T NO PLACE FOR LITTLE GIRLS.

I'VE HEARD STORIES. SO ARE YOU FOR HIRE OR NOT?

AND JUST 'OW DO YE FIGURE ON PAYIN' YER PASSAGE? WE TAKE *GOLD,* SWEETHEART, NOT MOONBEAMS AN' FAIRY DUST.

I HAVE MONEY. I SOLD A HORSE THIS MORNING. A WHITE CHARGER.

DID YE NOW? DON'T SUPPOSE IT'S ANY USE ASKIN' WHERE YE *GOT* SUCH A FINE ANIMAL?

I DON'T SUPPOSE IT IS.

HA! I LIKE THE CUT O' YER JIB, RED....

IF YE WANT TO TRY BUYIN' YER WAY ABOARD, YE'LL 'AVE TO TALK TO THE CAP'N.

THE BUCKLED SWASH

NO SCALLYWAGS

'E'S IN THE TAVERN YONDER.

GOES BY THE NAME O'....

17

19

SO YOU *DO* KNOW IT.

ONLY BY NAME. IT'S A LEGEND AMONG SAILORS.

SOME SAY A DEMON LIVES THERE. OTHERS SAY THERE'S RICHES BEYOND IMAGINATION...

...BUT NO ONE'S EVER ACTUALLY *SEEN* IT.

I'M NOT CERTAIN IT EVEN REALLY EXISTS.

IT DOES...

AT LEAST ON THIS MAP.

WHERE DID YOU GET—?

FROM THE PODHU HEALERS. THEY SEND CARRIER PIGEONS THERE.

FOR WHAT PURPOSE?

THAT'S WHAT I'D LIKE TO FIND OUT.

THE FIRST CARD IS THE *KNIGHT OF SWORDS.*

NO SURPRISE.... I COULD EASILY HAVE PREDICTED IT.

KNIGHT of SWORDS

THE KNIGHT IS *YOU,* OF COURSE.

HEH. IF THAT'S THE BEST YOU CAN DO, I'LL HAVE MY SHILLING BACK.

WE'VE ONLY JUST BEGUN, MY YOUNG FRIEND! THE KNIGHT OF SWORDS ALSO INDICATES *CHANGE.* IT PROMISES MUCH TO COME IN THE NEXT SIX CARDS.

LET US SEE WHAT THEY ARE....

23

VERY WELL, THEN.

WE MAY FIND NOTHING BUT EMPTY OCEAN, BUT I'LL BE HAPPY TO TAKE YOUR MONEY EITHER WAY.

ONE CONDITION, THOUGH...

SAILORS ARE OLD-FASHIONED. AND SUPERSTITIOUS. MY MEN WON'T TAKE KINDLY TO A GIRL ABOARD.

Z

WEAR THIS, AND TIE YOUR HAIR BACK.

IF ANYONE ASKS, YOU'RE A *BOY.* GOT IT?

I...I *GUESS...*

I COULD GO BY THE NAME *JARED.* IT'S MY BROTHER'S NAME.

WHATEVER.

24

WHICH BEGS THE QUESTION....AREN'T YOU AFRAID I'LL SIMPLY TAKE YOUR MONEY AND TURN YOU IN?

I THOUGHT ABOUT THAT....

....BUT I'M GUESSING THE TREASURES OF ASTAROTH ARE ENOUGH THAT YOU'D GAMBLE OUR BOUNTIES.

DON'T BE TOO SURE. *EASY* MONEY IS THE *BEST* MONEY....

....STILL, I HAD MY OWN CLOSE CALL WITH THOSE RED-CAPED DOGS LAST SUMMER, AND ONLY BARELY ESCAPED THE DUNGEON MYSELF.

I DON'T WANT TO RUN INTO THEM ANY MORE THAN YOU DO.

IN THAT CASE, WE'D BETTER FIND THE BACK DOOR....

26

ACT TWO

Tribes

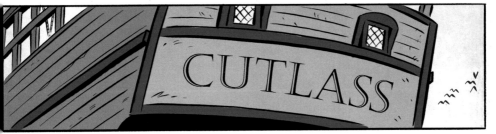

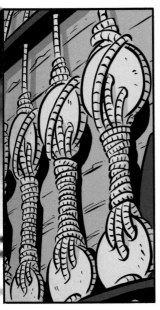

SHE'S...

HAPPY?

DESSA LOVES THE OPEN ROAD. EVEN IF THAT ROAD IS AN OCEAN.

I THINK SHE'S HAPPY 'CAUSE WE'RE GETTIN' CLOSER TO FINDIN' HER BROTHER.

YOU REALLY THINK WE'RE GONNA FIND ANYTHING ON THAT ISLAND? ASSUMING THERE EVEN *IS* AN ISLAND?

YOU *DON'T?*

OI!

YOU!

I REMEMBER HEARIN' 'BOUT YOU.

RUN OUTTA THE TRIBE FOR BEIN' A *ONE-HEADED FREAK.*

HEY, WHO YOU CALLING A FREAK?!

TRY LOOKING IN A *MIRROR* SOMETIME, SNAGGLE-FACE!

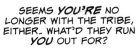

SEEMS **YOU'RE** NO LONGER WITH THE TRIBE, EITHER. WHAT'D THEY RUN **YOU** OUT FOR?

NOT FER BEIN' A FREAK WITH ONE HEAD, **THAT'S** FER SURE.

'EY!

YOU TWO!

STEP BACK FROM EACH OTHER, OR I'LL TELL THE CAP'N TO SHORT YER RUM RATION!

IF I 'AVE TO TELL YE AGAIN, IT'LL BE THE LASH FOR BOTH O' YE!

YOU HAVE NO TRIBE.

YOU'RE WRONG....

THOSE TWO ARE MY TRIBE NOW.

The EYE

HEH!

HOW FITTING!

DID I NOT ALREADY PREDICT THAT YOU ARE SEARCHING FOR SOMETHING? OR RATHER SOME*ONE*?

ARE YOU GOING TO TELL ME *ANYTHING* I DON'T ALREADY KNOW?

THE CARDS DO NOT LIE, AND NOR DOES OGHRA.

I ALREADY *HAVE*, IMPATIENT ONE! BECAUSE THE EYE ALSO REPRESENTS *HOPE*.

I PREDICT *SUCCESS* IN YOUR SEARCH.

34

THOUGH PERHAPS NOT THE ONE YOU THINK. AFTER ALL, DO ANY OF US *REALLY* KNOW WHAT WE'RE SEARCHING FOR?

ENOUGH RIDDLES. GET ON WITH IT.

VERY WELL.

KING OF CROWNS

THE *KING OF CROWNS,* INVERTED.

A KING WHO *ISN'T.*

THIS IS THE THING FOR WHICH YOU ARE SEARCHING.

THAT IS IN THE PAST.

NO.

IT IS THE *FUTURE.*

I THINK I'VE SPOTTED A SHIP!

THERE.

THREE POINTS OFF THE PORT QUARTER.

YOU'VE REALLY TAKEN TO THIS, DESSA. YOU'LL MAKE A SAILOR YET.

WHOSE FLAG IS SHE FLYING?

TO YOUR STATIONS, MEN! PIRATES OFF THE PORT QUARTER!

YE 'EARD 'IM, COCKLE-HEADS...TO YER POSTS!

I DON'T UNDERSTAND. AREN'T *YOU* A PIRATE?

BITE YOUR TONGUE! *I*, MY DEAR, AM A *SMUGGLER.*

THERE'S A DIFFERENCE?

I KNOW HOW TO USE THIS SWORD, BUT I AVOID TROUBLE IF I CAN. IT'S BAD FOR BUSINESS.

PIRATES *GO LOOKING* FOR TROUBLE.

SO WHAT DO WE DO?!

SHE'S A BIGGER SHIP THAN WE ARE. HEAVIER...

...WE *OUTRUN* HER.

SHE'S MOVING FAST FOR SUCH A BIG SHIP. WE NEED MORE SPEED.

DUE RESPECT, CAP'N, BUT WE'VE TRIMMED THE SAILS AS MUCH THEY'RE GONNA BE TRIMMED. AND WE CAN'T MAKE THE WIND BLOW 'ARDER.

NO...

...BUT WE CAN LIGHTEN THE SHIP. TELL THE MEN. ANY CARGO WE DON'T NEED GOES OVER THE SIDE.

BUT CAP'N...

THAT'S AN ORDER.

THE FOURTH CARD...

OH, MY... HOW VERY INTERESTING.

THE QUEEN OF CROWNS, ALSO INVERTED.

WHAT DO YOU READ INTO THAT, SOOTHSAYER?

I CAN TELL YOU ONLY THAT THIS CARD SYMBOLIZES SOMETHING YOU DO NOT EXPECT...

...A WOMAN OR GIRL WHO IS NOT WHAT SHE SEEMS.

41

AND THE FIFTH CARD?

LET US SEE...

The LOVERS

I'M TO MARRY, I SUPPOSE?

NO.

INVERTED, THE LOVERS SUGGEST *SECRETS.* THIS CARD REPRESENTS THOSE AROUND YOU...

DECEPTION IS AT HAND.

THEM BLOODY PIRATES IS STILL GAININ', CAP'N!

THEY MUST HAVE DUMPED THEIR OWN CARGO OVERNIGHT, KNOWING WE'D DO THE SAME. HE'S **SMART**, WHOEVER HE IS.

I GUESS THAT'S WHY 'E'S THE KING.

HE'S DETERMINED, AT THE VERY LEAST. WE'VE SEEN ANY NUMBER OF OTHER SHIPS THAT MIGHT HAVE CAUGHT HIS EYE. BIGGER ONES, TOO.

SO WHY'S 'E AFTER **US?**

FAIR ENOUGH. BUT WHY SEND *US?*

ER... THE CAP'N FIGURED YOU'D WANT A CHANCE TO STRETCH YER LEGS, NOT BEIN' ACCUSTOMED TO SEA TRAVEL AN' WHATNOT.

ALL RIGHT....

BETTER GET STARTED, THEN. IT'LL BE AN ADVENTURE.

SURE—BECAUSE WE DON'T HAVE ENOUGH OF *THOSE.*

QUIET, YOU.

LEAD ON, TULLY.

MY SINCEREST APOLOGIES, YOU THREE...!

BUT HAVING YOU ABOARD IS SIMPLY TOO DANGEROUS!

YOU'RE BETTER OFF ON THAT ISLAND THAN IN THE HANDS OF THE PIRATE KING, I ASSURE YOU!

YOU COULD ALMOST SAY I'M DOING YOU A FAVOR!

OF COURSE, IT'S NOT THE ISLAND YOU *WANTED*...

...BUT REST ASSURED THAT WHILE I'M SPENDING THE TREASURE OF ASTAROTH, I'LL REMEMBER YOU WARMLY!

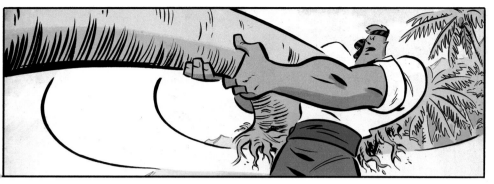

WHAP

THANKS,
PAL!

!?!

UP ANCHOR!

ALL HANDS, PREPARE TO MAKE SAIL!

FISK!

THEY'RE GETTING AWAY!

HNHHH!

WHA—?!

WHUMP

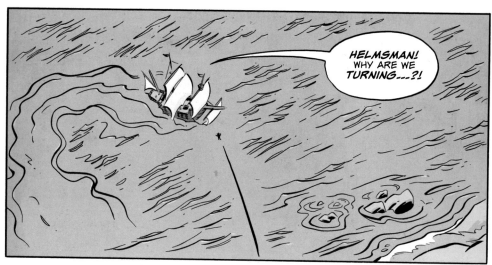

POINT US OUT TO SEA, FOOL! WE'RE GOING TO RUN AGROUND!

I...I'M *TRYIN'*, CAP'N...!

THE RUDDER SEEMS TO BE *STUCK!*

THEN GET IT *UNSTUCK!* BEFORE I FEED YOU TO THE SHARKS!

LET'S SEE...

BY THE GREAT MERMAID!

I'LL FIX YOU, LITTLE WRETCH...

SLICE

SWISH

SWIPE

ziiiip

OW!

YOU...!

CAN'T STAY
AND CHAT,
MUTTON
HEADS...

61

...GOT A BOAT TO ANCHOR!

SPLOOOSH

Creak!

WHA—?!

OOF!

YOU....!

SORRY, QUINN...

ACT THREE

The King Who Isn't

A WARNING, MY FRIEND...

...THE FINAL TWO CARDS WILL SHOW *THE ROAD AHEAD.* OBSTACLES YOU WILL FACE, AND THEIR OUTCOME.

DO NOT MAKE ME GO FURTHER UNLESS YOU TRULY WISH TO KNOW YOUR FATE.

WILL YOU RETURN MY COIN?

NO REFUNDS, I'M AFRAID.

THEN PROCEED.

69

NOW WHAT?!

GIVE ME THE MAP AND FREE TOPPER, AND I'LL TELL FISK TO PUT US DOW—

POOM!

ATTENTION, CREW OF THE **CUTLASS!**

THAT WAS BUT A WARNING!

PUT THE SHIP DOWN, DROP YOUR WEAPONS, AND PREPARE TO BE BOARDED BY THE **KING OF PIRATES!**

SO THAT'S IT, THEN?

I'M TO DIE AT THE GALLOWS?

HEH. NO.

WELL, PERHAPS. THE HANGED MAN REPRESENTS *SACRIFICE*.

MY OWN? OR SOMEONE ELSE'S?

ONE OR THE OTHER. PERHAPS BOTH.

YOU'RE HEDGING.

I'M NOT.

TURN THE LAST CARD.

GIVE ME THE MAP.

THE.... THE MAP?

ANYTHING YOU SAY, MASTER PIRATE KING.... SIR.

I'LL ALSO HAVE *THIS* BACK.

<GASP!>

YOU....! THE TAVERN!

YOU NEED TO BE MORE CAREFUL WHERE YOU TELL YOUR SECRETS, GIRL...

AND *TO WHOM.*

I'VE LEARNED THAT LESSON *ALREADY,* BELIEVE ME.

SHALL WE LOAD THEIR CARGO, M'LORD?

THE FOOLS THREW MOST OF IT IN THE OCEAN. I HAVE EVERYTHING I CAME FOR.

BUT THE FUGITIVES... THE REWARD MONEY!

IF THE DARK ISLAND CONTAINS HALF THE RICHES THEY SAY, WE'LL NOT WANT FOR SILVER OR GOLD EVER AGAIN, WYETH.

CONSIDER YOURSELVES FORTUNATE, SMUGGLERS! NOT MANY ENCOUNTER THE PIRATE KING AND LEAVE WITH THEIR SHIP INTACT!

OR WITH THEIR LIVES, FOR THAT MATTER!

BUT IF I THOUGHT THERE WAS ANY CHANCE YOU'D BE ABLE TO FOLLOW US IN THIS RICKETY OLD PIECE OF DRIFTWOOD, YOU WOULDN'T BE SO LUCKY!

HEH.

I'LL LEAVE YOU WITH A WORD OF ADVICE...

PUT *THIS ONE* IN CHARGE.

SHE'S GOT *TWICE* THE SPIRIT THE REST OF YOU HAVE.

HA!

A *GIRL* CAPTAIN?!

I'D *DIE* FIRST!

I ASSURE YOU, ETTIN...

79

I'VE HAD A CHANGE OF HEART, WYETH. BRING THE GIRL AND HER TWO COMPANIONS. THEY WILL TRAVEL WITH US AS MY GUESTS.

YES, M'LADY.

BESIDES, I SUSPECT THEIR BUSINESS ON THE ISLAND OF ASTAROTH WON'T INTERFERE WITH *OURS.*

IF THERE'S TREASURE, IT'S ALL YOURS. I'M JUST LOOKING FOR MY TWIN BROTHER.

THEN MAY WE *BOTH* FIND WHAT WE SEEK.

WHAT IS THE MEANING OF THIS?

I THINK THAT, LIKE THE FIRST CARD, THIS ONE REPRESENTS *YOU*...

YOU CALL ME A *FOOL?*

NOT AT ALL, GOOD SIR...

THE FOOL IS A *WILD CARD.* IT SIMPLY MEANS THAT YOUR FATE CANNOT BE PREDICTED.

IN THE END, SOMETIMES IT IS OUR CHOICES AND THE UNPREDICTABILITY OF CHANCE THAT RULE OUR LIVES...

...PERHAPS EVEN AS MUCH AS OUR STARS.

GOD'S TEETH! YOUR PREDICTION IS THAT *YOU CAN'T PREDICT ANYTHING?!*

I'M A FOOL, ALL RIGHT. YOU'RE NOTHING BUT A SIDESHOW HUCKSTER, AFTER ALL.

I'LL HAVE THAT SHILLING BACK.

NO REFU—

NOW.

FOLD YOUR TENT AND BE GONE...

WHUMP

...BEFORE MY *BOOT* FINDS YOUR *BACKSIDE.*

84

85

SO, IT'S REALLY THERE?

RIGHT WHERE YOUR MAP SAID IT WOULD BE.

WE'VE LEFT ALL OTHER SHIPS BEHIND. EVEN *I'VE* NEVER BEEN THIS FAR OUT TO SEA.

I DON'T SEE IT...

NOT THERE, CHILD...

UP THERE.

GOD'S TEETH!

87

I'VE BEEN AT SEA MY WHOLE LIFE, AND HAVE NEVER SEEN ANYTHING LIKE IT.

WHO COULD HAVE **BUILT** SUCH A THING?

HIS NAME IS **GREYFALCON.** THE MAN WHO TOOK MY BROTHER AWAY.

THIS IS WHERE HE TOOK HIM. I DON'T KNOW WHY.

BUT JARED IS HERE, I KNOW IT...

MY BROTHER IS UP THERE, RIGHT NOW.

I CAN **FEEL** IT.

89

WHAT IN THE SIX KINGDOMS HAS BEEN KEEPING YOU?

PHINEAS!

I...I'M SORRY, CAPTAIN.

BUT THIS MAN SAYS HE HAS A HORSE WORTHY OF YOU, AND IS WILLING TO MAKE A GOOD PRICE ON IT.

INDEED, SIR. WE'RE JUST WAITING FOR MY BOY TO BRING HER AROUND.

FINE, THEN. LET US HOPE HE DOESN'T TARRY MUCH LONGER...

I'VE ALREADY WASTED MORE THAN ENOUGH TIME TODAY.

WHY, HERE HE IS NOW...

Don't miss the sixth book in the Three Thieves series — coming soon!

As Dessa, Topper and Fisk begin to unravel the mysteries of Astaroth, they encounter surprises and setbacks around every corner. Captain Drake, meanwhile, hopes Jared will help lead him to Dessa, but the boy only lands him in hot water with the rest of the Queen's Dragons.

With more thrills, escapes, traps and intrigue than ever before, this penultimate chapter in the Three Thieves series has both Dessa and Captain Drake wondering if they've been headed down the wrong path since the first step of the journey.

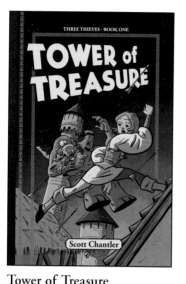

Tower of Treasure

HC 978-1-55453-414-2 • $17.95
PB 978-1-55453-415-9 • $8.95

★ Winner of the Joe Shuster Award, Comics for Kids

★ "Thrilling action sequences that don't sacrifice sense for sizzle ... the kind of fantasy tale that can be relished by children of all ages."
— *Quill & Quire,* starred review

"An entertaining and action packed new fantasy adventure series."
— *Publishers Weekly*

The Sign of the Black Rock

HC 978-1-55453-416-6 • $17.95
PB 978-1-55453-417-3 • $8.95

"An animated, breathlessly paced adventure that's just hitting its stride."
— *Kirkus Reviews*

"Touches of zany slapstick balance nicely with Dessa's continued resolve to find her lost brother, and Chantler's inviting cartooning captures it all with special aplomb."
— *Booklist*

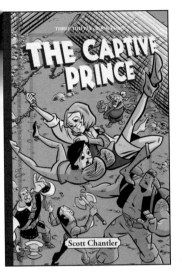

The Captive Prince

HC 978-1-55453-776-1 • $17.95
PB 978-1-55453-777-8 • $8.95

"Nary a dull moment, nor even a slow one in this escapade's latest outing."
— *Kirkus Reviews*

"Heaps of charm … snappy, colorful artwork … this one can stand well on its own, though it successfully expands on the growing epic."
— *Booklist*

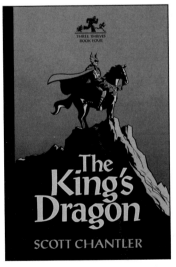

The King's Dragon

HC 978-1-55453-778-5 • $17.95
PB 978-1-55453-779-2 • $8.95

"Chantler's cartooning remains sharp, lively, and inviting, and his eye for rousing action sequences is top-notch. But it's his skill as a writer that shines through."
— *Booklist*

"In his cleanly drawn action sequences, Chantler ingeniously links present and past with parallel acts or dialogue … adds further depth to a particularly well-wrought tale."
— *Kirkus Reviews*